Even Gandhi Got Hungry and Buddha Got Mad

Nanice Ellis

www.Nanice.com

978-1517106546
Amazon Edition

Designed By ECKO Publishing
9587 So. Grandview Dr.
Salt Lake City, UT 84092
1.800.614.3578
www.ECKOPublishing.com

www.Nanice.com

In every moment, you have the opportunity to experience and express your greatest spiritual self, just by being fully present, without story, in the every day chaos, challenge and gift, of the life you are now living. This is your invitation.....

A Book About You!

This is not a book about Gandhi or Buddha. It is a book about you and your spiritual journey through an often chaotic world. It is a book that offers unconditional acceptance for you, right now, no matter where you are on your spiritual, or not so spiritual, path.

This book gives you permission to re-define your life, according to what you want and desire. It takes away the rules, regulations and pressures of how you thought it had to be and hands the reins of your life, back to you. It will help you understand that you have created your life and you can re-create it any way you want it. But, most of all, I hope it reminds you that the journey of your life is a gift and like any gift, it deserves to be cherished and enjoyed in every possible way. This is your divine invitation, to relax and remember who you really are and most of all, to enjoy this great adventure that you yourself created and can re-create as often as you desire.

What do you dream possible?

Contents

CONTENTS

RE-DEFINING SPIRITUALITY IN THE 21ST CENTURY

...why would my soul choose to have this human experience in the first place, if the goal was to avoid the experience?

Driving down I-15 in Salt Lake City, Utah, I fantasized about running away from everything. I'd take my kids and all I could fit into my Lincoln Navigator and go find a small cabin in the woods, in some remote area. It would be a place where I could breathe and think and meditate - a place where I could explore my spirituality, without distraction and without having to answer to the constant demands of anxious voices in my head. I just wanted peace, and it seemed to be moving further and further away every day of my life. The more I worked to get it, the more it teased me and lured me down a confusing and distracting path. I believed that in order to re-find my spiritual path, I needed to move away from the hectic life I created.

I must admit, just years before, I had moved to Salt Lake City to escape from the chaos and stress of New York; but somehow, just a few years later, I found myself in just as much mental and emotional confusion as I had experienced living in New York. And now, with 3 kids and being a single mom, there was even more stress. So, as I drove along the freeway, I dreamt of a life much simpler.

I'd wake up every morning and be able to meditate. I'd take time for a healthy breakfast with my kids and then, we would go on our daily hike, through the woods, stopping to listen for the birds sweet songs, or to smell the fragrant flowers. We'd take our time, because there would not be any schedule to follow or anyone to answer to. Once back at the cabin, I'd be able to write for hours, knocking out one book after another, and most of all, there would be plenty of time for my spiritual growth. The days would continue to flow peacefully, just like that. What I didn't consider was that my spirit needs variety and challenge to grow – how long would it be until boredom set in, my kids drove me crazy because of their own and, without life experience, how could I grow, and what would I find to write about? Isn't it the living of life that offers us wisdom to grow and to share?

I never did run away and find that cabin in the woods. Instead, I stopped resisting the story of my life, and I reclaimed my spirituality, in the middle of my *made-up chaos*.

Maybe, in another time and place, great spiritual beings went off to mountain tops to meditate and become one with God. It's said that, some of them even lost control of their physical bodies, and had to be fed, cared for bodily, and maybe, even had to have their asses wiped. No matter how much I wanted to be a great spiritual leader, there was no way that I was going to have someone wipe my ass. So, what did that mean? That meant that I was going to have to find another way. It meant I was going to have to re-define spirituality and what it meant to me. Could it also mean that I would have to embrace the fact that I was a human? It sure seemed like it – there didn't seem a reasonable or acceptable way for me to avoid it; and even if I could avoid the pitfalls and downfalls of being a human, why would my soul choose to have this human experience in the first place, if the goal was to avoid the experience?

I realized that the key to experiencing my spirituality, was not in evolving and overcoming the flesh. It was in embracing it - embracing the humanness of who I am. Embracing my shortcomings, my fears and all the parts of me that I was still working on. It meant accepting my inability to walk across the street without sometimes falling, my strange way of laughing with one eye closed and all the faux pas of my life. Like the time, I backed up and totaled the car behind me – in my driveway. The times I got frustrated at my kids, instead of taking the high road. And then there was the time I had a food fight with my mother and smashed an over-ripe tomato in her white hair. I could spend my whole life trying to overcome my humanness so that I could become a better person and evolve spiritually but, let's face it, how can you evolve, when you are denying and judging the experience of what is – the experience of your humanness. Knowing your spiritual self happens in the moment, and if we are always judging and resisting the moment, how can we experience who we really are, or the fullness of life for that matter?

Awakening our inner selves happens as a result of embracing and loving our humanness, despite our perceived flaws and faults. It means laughing at our shortcomings – not out of judgment, but out of a true appreciation for the challenges of being human, and a lightheartedness that comes from understanding that there is no judge or jury – and that the purpose of life is simply what we make it to be.

Your Grand Adventure

*Enlightenment is inevitable,
but living life, to the fullest, is optional.*

You are a beautiful and perfect spiritual being, just the way you are. You don't have to prove or change a thing. You already possess everything that you have spent your entire life striving to attain.

If we already have everything contained within our greatest selves, and we are perfect, powerful, all-knowing beings, why would we choose to be human? It is the same reason that we go to the movies; to experience – to feel – to observe – to be a part of a grand and unique adventure called "our lives". We powerful beings have chosen this mighty, challenging human experience, simply to have another grand adventure. There is no destination, reward or great prize at the end of the journey. *The journey is the prize.* The journey of our lives, *is* the gift and we have the freedom to use that gift any way we desire. The only limits to what we can choose and experience, are the limits that our minds create, and the illusions of scarcity that keep us feeling small and powerless.

There is no right or wrong way to live your life – there is no final destination where you will be rewarded or punished for what you did or didn't do. Your life is the unfolding of your ability to experience everything there is to experience, and to participate in all aspects of the human adventure.

No matter what you do, you are a spiritual being, having a human experience. You could go off and meditate on a mountain top, for the rest of your life, and become one with God, and that would be wonderful, but if your soul came here to enjoy and participate in this grand adventure of life, wouldn't it be a waste, if you denied yourself this amazing experience – this gift of life and living. No matter how you choose to experience and express your spirituality, you are no less spiritual.

Spirituality is not only something that happens when we are peaceful and in touch with God. Spirituality is forever happening in

the day to day experience of our lives. The full engagement, in life, is what brings us to the knowing of our power, and the truth of who we are. When we deny the human adventure, and hide our creative desires, we deny one of the greatest experiences of our spirituality.

Observing life, from the side-lines, is fine, but if the journey of your life is a gift of grand adventure, what might you be missing every time fear stops you from making a move, every time you're stuck because of your uncertainty, every time you want something but are afraid to ask, every time you want to love and be loved but instead you hide beneath unhealthy habits and behaviors that seem to keep you safe from getting hurt. Do you want to know who you really are, and the magnificence you are capable of? Then, you must start living your life to the fullest possible capacity – every day – without excuse, apology or shame.

You came here for one thing – to experience life, by expressing the fullness of who you really are. You can't do this by hiding in an emotional basement. You can only experience your life and the possibilities of what you can create, by fully embarking on the journey, and becoming present in your current life.

- *Decide what works for you and what doesn't.*
- *Choose the people you want to spend your precious time with.*
- *Explore your hidden creativity.*
- *Stop doing things because you have to, or should.*
- *Start doing things because you want to and it feels good.*
- *Still the ego-mind as much as you can.*
- *Listen to your intuition, and the higher guidance of your divine self.*
- *Stop playing roles in your life, just because you are trying to get your emotional needs met.*
- *Be at choice in all areas of your life – no matter what.*
- *Act as if you are the sole creator of your life – because you are.*

You have been given this grand gift of life, and it is up to you to create and experience whatever you choose to think into creation.

What grand possibility or adventure might you manifest, in order to experience your life, to the fullest possible magnitude?

PERFECTING SPIRITUALITY

Your Greatest Spiritual Moment is NOW.

Why is it that we think we have to be and act a certain way, in order to be spiritual? And, when we fail to meet that made-up definition, we beat ourselves up with guilt, shame, and maybe even fear of karma. We've been brain-washed to believe that we must be and act a certain way in order to be spiritual - or even express our spirituality. Ironically, the concept of spiritual perfection actually disconnects us from experiencing our spiritual selves.

Spiritual Myth -
There is only one way to be spiritual

Spirituality happens in every moment of every day, without having to adhere to any spiritual guidelines in order *to be* spiritual or become one with God. You are already one with God.

Every time you judge yourself or strive for some idea of spiritual perfection, (only to fail and then judge yourself miserably), you move further away from the knowing of your divinity. There is no one right or wrong way to be spiritual, and no matter what your definition is, there will be many times when you fail to meet it, but, that doesn't make you any less spiritual. The judgment of yourself will, however, disconnect you from *experiencing* your spiritual self.

What is your definition of spirituality? Is it a reasonable definition that works with your life? Or, does it stop you from living fully, in the moment, by causing internal mental beatings? For me, being spiritual meant being a kind and loving person always – no matter what. It meant forgiving, instead of being angry and never ever judging anybody. And when I strayed away from this ideal, which seemed to be more often than I'd like to admit, I internally beat myself up by feeling bad and judging myself. I also stopped trusting myself, and how I would behave in the world. How could it be that my intentions were of the highest good, yet it was so easy to fail? Was I not a good enough spiritual student, seeker, or teacher?

The truth is that living a spiritual life does not happen only in the moments of being kind, loving, and forgiving. It happens in all moments. It is not an experience that happens only during meditation, praying, or doing good deeds. It happens during screaming, torturous childbirth. It happens when you have a fight with your best friend, because she (or you) did the unspeakable. It happens when the neighbor's 150 pound dog poops on your lawn, every day, and you want revenge. It happens. It just is. You can't do anything to live the spiritual life. You also can't stop it. No matter what your life consists of right now, it's spiritual – poop and all. The pressure, to live the *right* spiritual path, is off.

Love is not more spiritual than hate. Kindness is not more spiritual than telling someone to "get lost". How can any interpretation of God, not be God? It's all spiritual, and you get to decide how you want to express and experience your spirituality, every moment of every day, and no matter what you decide for that moment, it's all good – no one is judging you. When the pressure is off, it is easier to authentically return to a state of love and expressing love.

Even quantum physicists today know that we are all made up from the same energy, and they are beginning to refer to it as God. Does that God energy change from someone who is good to someone we would deem bad? No, it is the same energy. Does it change when you are reaching your spiritual ideals, and when you fail miserably? It is still the same. So, if it is all God energy, how can anything or anyone or any act not be spiritual? It is. You are.

The *experience of our spirituality* happens when we are fully present, but if we are only present when life meets our ideal, we miss not only the experience of spirituality, but we also miss most of our lives. If we are completely present with acceptance and even gratitude, every moment holds the possibility of enlightenment, and the true knowing of self.

What is your definition of spirituality?

How can you shift your spiritual ideals, in such a way, that they support your life and growth?

Your only Judge and Jury is You!

You are the powerful God that you have been praying to – to answer all your prayers

There is only one being to answer to, and there is only one being controlling your life. That being is you. There is no one, up above, judging or punishing you for what you have done or not done. Your life is your canvas, and you can paint on it exactly what you wish. No matter what you may have believed or believe now, there are no rules, except the ones you create and believe in, or give others the power to create for you. You are the ruler and creator of your life.

Everything you see around you is your glorious creation. Maybe, you don't like what you see, or maybe you don't know how you created it. Nevertheless, you are the creator, and if you don't like what you see, or what you have, then re-create something else.

You might be thinking "even if no one is judging me, *what about karma"*?

Spiritual Myth -
I must be good or I will create bad karma for myself.

Karma is not a punishment for good or bad doings – in fact, karma, the way we know it, does not exist. We don't get good karma for doing good or bad karma for doing bad, as we've been taught. If that were the case, even the best of us would find ourselves in the endless cycle of trying to make up for our less-than-perfect behavior. So, what then is karma? Karma is the energy we put out in our thoughts and the manifestations those thoughts create. Simply stated, karma is a return on our mental investment in thought and energy. Wherever we focus energy and emotion, that energy and emotion returns to us in the things we manifest and attract. If you want to shift "bad karma", simply move your thoughts and feelings to focus on what you do want. In other words, internally align yourself energetically with whatever you desire. Internally, align yourself with whatever you consider "good karma".

Our thoughts are like magnets and will attract to us whatever we focus on – especially those things we focus on repetitively. If you want to know what goes on in someone's mind, simply look at their life. Life is a physical manifestation of the thoughts we think, and the feelings we feel every day.

This means that you are responsible for everything in your life – the things you like and the things you don't like. The good news is, if we created everything around us, it means we can re-create our lives with consciousness and intention – we can create the lives we truly want to live, and no one and nothing can stop us.

To create our lives consciously, we must first know what we want, and have an understanding that, by dreaming it and feeling how it feels to experience it, we are creating it. It also means that we must de-focus energy from the things in our lives that we don't want. In other words, we must stop giving meaning to anything and everything that doesn't fit in with our greatest desires. Every time we give meaning to something, we give energy to it and we add to the reality of its existence. We are actually telling the universe to bring us more of the thing we are focusing on through the meaning we give it. If your neighbor appears to be ignoring you, and you tell yourself that people don't like you, or everybody is so rude, you will attract more situations where you can apply the same meaning. Most of the time, the meaning we give something is not even true.

The stories we tell ourselves seem to be a result of what we perceive in the outside world, and we are just interpreting reality. But, the truth is that we first make up the stories in our minds, and the world obliges us by making our stories the reality we then perceive through our senses. When we have evidence, of our stories, by what we experience, we further make up more stories to support our beliefs. The cycle never ends until we start taking responsibility for everything in our lives, and we change the stories we tell ourselves.

It's not easy to change our stories and create new meaning when the world is screaming negativity at us. Sometimes, it even seems impossible, but if you keep reacting to external experiences, by giving them negative meaning, you will forever be re-creating exactly what you don't want.

You are the creator of your life. You are the only one doing it. There's no one to blame or thank. It is you. If you don't like what you see, then dream a new dream, and stop giving power and meaning to the old one. It's not easy, but it is the only thing that makes sense because, no matter how hard you want something or work for it, it will not come, if your thoughts and feelings are not completely in alignment – if you are not internally in alignment with what you want.

You are the powerful God that you have been praying to – to answer all your prayers. It's time to start answering your own prayers, by getting your thoughts, feelings, and the stories you tell, in alignment with what you really want. Every time you question your story, or the meaning you give to an experience, you begin to break down your current reality – you stop giving energy to it. Every time you tell yourself a story which brings you joy, peace and happiness, you begin to create a new reality, which supports your greatest dreams.

You can have it all – and you deserve it. There are no conditions on how much you deserve. If you desire it, you deserve it. No questions asked. You get to fulfill every wish and dream, simply by creating thoughts, feelings and stories, which manifest the reality you desire and deserve.

If you found a magic lamp and could make any number of wishes for anything and everything you wanted, without limitations, what would you wish for?

What thoughts, feelings and affirming stories do you need to create within yourself, to manifest your wish list?

YOU ARE...

What lies within –
manifests in reality!

Just like Buddha, Gandhi and all the great spiritual leaders, you are created from the God-force of all. You, and everything around you, are God's energy, and that energy does not change, no matter what you do or don't do – you may not know how to utilize this energy, or how to be inspired by this energy, but it is always available. It is this creative force that makes you the great creator you are.

As great creators, we have the ability to manifest all we desire, by simply changing the density of energy, with our thoughts, feelings and focus. We have the ability to alter the vibration of all energy, with the use of our powerful minds. Water can become vapor or ice, but it is still water; it is affected by an influence other than itself. The energy did not change – only the density, or vibration, and once changed, it is not locked into the new form – with another outside influence of heat or cold, it can change again, but it will always remain the energy of water.

It is the same with us. The energy remains constant – we are always God's energy; but we can alter the density or vibration with our thoughts, feelings and intentions. This is the secret formula to creating what you want. This is what manifests in our lives, and what makes us the way we are. Most of us have forgotten that we possess the magic to create and re-create our lives, and that even now, in our amnesia, we are creating.

If you were to awaken to the powerful truth of who you really are right now, how would that affect your spiritual identity? Would you suddenly be able to take responsibility for every area of your life? Would you be able to forgive all those you once believed hurt you? Would you start laughing at all the things you once took so seriously?

The only difference between you and the greatest spiritual beings of all times is that they woke up and remembered who they really were. Waking up is inevitable so there's no rush or pressure and certainly no need to judge yourself. And maybe the fastest and easiest route to awakening is enjoying the dream – that you yourself created on some yet unconscious level.

If you want to know what you have created, look at the mirror of your life. Without judgment, describe your creations:

____

____

____

____

____

____

Now describe what you want to create:

____

____

____

____

____

____

____

What do you need to do, to become internally in alignment, with that which you desire?

Spiritual Roller Coaster!

There is no difference between being human and dreaming at night – and being God and dreaming the life you are having.

Awakening, to the truth, doesn't mean that we suddenly glide through life, without challenge or mishap. It doesn't even mean that we live the rest of our lives in a state of peace, love and joy. For most of us humans on this **roller coaster ride called "LIFE"**, it is filled with ups and downs and bends and grinds in the road. It is anything but stable and predictable. One day you have an amazing epiphany and believe that you have spiritually arrived, and that for the rest of your life you will be unaffected by the eventful happenings around you. Maybe, this state lasts for a few hours, days, or weeks, and if you are really lucky, for months, but for most of us humans, it is only a temporary state, and somehow we get dragged back into the drama of our lives – the interpretation of experience. We then wonder, what happened to that great epiphany? Was it real? How did I lose it? - And most importantly, how do I get it back? Sometimes, we even lose that spiritual state for years, and doubt it will ever return. We meditate, read, pray, twist ourselves into yoga knots and maybe even renounce our humanness or sex in the search for that blissful spiritual state. Nothing seems to work! Damn it! Then, one day, almost out of the blue, another epiphany occurs – and it's back! This time we cherish it and try desperately to hold on to it, but once again, it elusively flies off somewhere, as soon as life gets in the way. So, you ask yourself, "How can I regain and retain my spiritual center – my spiritual state of peace and bliss, when I have a life to live?" This is the challenge and grand adventure that you and I have the amazing and rare opportunity to master – this is the journey of the *modern-day-seeker*.

Spiritual Myth -
Once you are enlightened - you're done!

What most spiritual leaders fail to share with us modern day seekers is that spiritual evolution is not like a ladder, where you reach one level and then climb to the next. It's much more like a roller coaster. You have great ups and great downs; and sometimes you even loop around and around, and find yourself upside down, with vomit moving

up from your gut. At some point, we all wake up and realize that we are the ones controlling the roller coaster, and we can get off or change the ride; but, until then, for most of us, we go along for the ride, experiencing one great awakening, and then getting caught up in the story of our lives once again. We keep repeating this pattern over and over.

There is no "getting it right" – there just "is". What's to get right, when you are a great powerful being, having an interesting and exciting adventure? We don't try to get our night time dreams "right". We just enjoy them or try to interpret them. I've never met someone who said "okay, I'm going to have the *right* dream tonight". There is no difference between being human and dreaming at night – and being God and dreaming the life you are having.

Spiritual ups and downs are natural, and it doesn't mean that you are doing anything wrong, or even that you necessarily have to do something different. When I used to experience a spiritual "down" after a spiritual "up" or, awakening, I felt that I lost something; maybe, I did something wrong, and I wondered if it would ever return. Sometimes, I went years, before the next spiritual high. But, having enough ups and downs, I began to realize that it was the "spiritual downs" – the times that I faced a challenge or got caught up in an issue – that empowered me to reach the next spiritual high. And, when I reached the next spiritual plateau, it was even higher than the one before. Not only had I retained the knowingness and awareness of prior spiritual peaks, I had somehow been building on them, in my times of being lost and distressed. Once I realized this, I stopped expecting the spiritual highs to last. I embraced them and enhanced them, when they came, but, like good friends who only come to visit on special occasions, I anticipated and accepted that once again they would leave when it was time. When the spiritual bottom fell out, I also had faith that whatever I was experiencing, however, "off the path" I seemed to have fallen (even to myself), that somehow I was still on the path, and I would emerge once again at another peak, even more spiritually enlightened than the time before. And, that it was in those greatest times of distress, and feeling most lost, that I was gaining the most momentum to propel me to another great spiritual high – it was then that I was growing and awakening.

This shift, in my awareness, has allowed me to be as grateful for the valleys of despair as the

peaks of greatest awareness. Instead of judging those incredible "unspiritual" experiences and my "unspiritual" responses to them, I embrace them with interest and intrigue. I wonder how it all fits together, and what I will learn in "this experience". I no longer wonder how or when the next spiritual high will happen. I know it will, and it somehow doesn't even matter anymore. The journey through the valley has become the gift and my gratitude lies not in the outcome, but in the experience of what is.

Map out the spiritual journey of your life; what challenging events have precipitated your spiritual awakenings?

On The Path Again....

Although I didn't understand every thing that was happening, my spiritual awakening began when I was about 11 years old. At that time, I become a vegetarian, started doing yoga, meditating and reading every spiritual and metaphysical book that I could get my hands on. I was the only kid in junior high, walking around the halls reading books on astral projection and re-incarnation. It certainly didn't do much for my social life.

Being an only child, and not having the social skills to maintain childhood friendships, I spent a lot of time alone in my head. As each attempt to make connections failed, I turned more and more inward. Every time I was rejected by classmates or the neighborhood kids, I would retreat to the kitchen in my home, and sit in the corner beside the refrigerator, and I would talk silently to the mop. Sadly, the mop became my best friend. But, it was also in those painful times that I started asking myself some profound questions. True,

I spent many years feeling sorry for myself and creating "poor me" stories, which the world obediently confirmed, but I also started getting some powerful answers to my questions. It took years to fully understand the answers, but the seed was planted and beginning to sprout in new upward directions. Around the age of 11, my mind was developed enough to grasp the very beginnings of understanding, and I was also old enough to take out books, on my own, from the public library.

In hindsight, I was so lucky to experience isolation and suffering, at an early age, because it made me start looking for answers and helped me to become aware of my spiritual path, years before I otherwise might have. It was truly a blessing.

Everyone's awareness of their spiritual path begins differently, and many people never become aware of it at all – that's okay too – they are no less spiritual. For most people who become "spiritual seekers", the journey begins because of some sort of pain that they are trying to escape from, or because of some questions they are trying to find answers to. By trying to overcome the pain and find happiness, they start asking profound questions and looking actively for answers. Many

of these questions and answers eventually lead to what we call the spiritual path. In other words, the pain and "unspiritual" crap precipitates the quest for knowing our spiritual essence. Without pain and suffering, we may never seek answers, and start asking the questions that lead to spiritual freedom and conscious living.

So, if it's our pain, suffering, and feelings like hate, fear, jealousy, and lack of trust and faith, that so often drives us to find answers on the spiritual path, how can we judge these "unspiritual experiences" and "unspiritual feelings" that lead us there? Without them, we might never remember who we really are. Is it possible that the worst moments of your life were really the best because they empowered you to start looking for more profound answers, uncovered your life's purpose, or opened up doors of understanding that had been previously hidden? Could it be that the challenges we face really are miracles in disguise?

What events in your life have guided or pushed you on your spiritual path?

Who would you be now, without the painful and "unspiritual experiences" of your life?

How is it possible that a situation, that you are now experiencing, will lead you to the answers you seek?

How might a current challenge be a gift, in disguise?

A State of Amnesia

Let us approach the journey of our lives, with a sense of fun and adventure, knowing that one day we will wake up and remember that this is what we intended in the first place.

Is it possible to have a grand and authentic adventure here on earth, when we remember that we created it? At first, we did remember and we knew we were Gods in human form but, as great creators, what we created seemed so real that we started identifying with the illusion (dream) and forgot that we created it in the first place (how amusing); but, this also served a purpose. As we got carried away with the illusion, and forgot our true identity, we were able to experience more and more of the adventure, through our emotions. Let's face it, a movie is less powerful than real life, only because, during the movie, a part of us always remembers that it is not real and not happening to us. If we believed that it was real and happening to us, our experience would be intensified. When we get swept away with an experience, that's where the grand adventure happens.

But what is the meaning of this adventure?

Our souls came here to experience all that is possible to experience in the human form – love, peace, joy, freedom; but how can we experience these wonderful things without first experiencing their contrast – without knowing the opposite. If you were to only know light and never darkness, how would you know what light is? If you only experience love – the true nature of who you really are, how would you know what love is? Could you know freedom, if you didn't experience imprisonment of some sort? In order to know something, we must have contrast and experience its opposite. This grand planet of Earth gives us the opportunity to experience love, joy, peace and freedom, by also offering the opportunity to experience the opposite. Therefore, all experiences are spiritual including hate, fear, sadness and everything else you and I have ever experienced. They are all an aspect of *all that is* and they all lead home to our true nature of love, which is never compromised in our sometimes long and arduous journey.

The question is not whether we will experience hate, anger or sadness during our lifetimes, the question is how long until we make another choice? In the process of experiencing life and all emotions, we get trapped in a perpetual state of attracting the same experiences to us, over and over again, by the stories we tell ourselves and the meanings we give them. We believe that we are victims of experience, when, in fact, we are attracting these experiences to us by our beliefs and the unconscious magnet in our minds. By identifying with stories that can last lifetimes, we reproduce those stories over and over again in the world – just as if we had unconsciously commanded.

At any time, you can end the cycle and reclaim your true eternal self and return home to a state of love and peace. From this true state of being, you can continue the journey here on earth and experience beauty beyond anything you could imagine. Without the need to feel a lower vibration of emotions, you are free to be present and when you are present, you will know the genius and magnificence of this world. Instead of battling with your inner stories, which have dragged you back into the same old creation, over and over again, you get to discover yourself, as an all powerful creator of your life and all that is.

We are not here to *learn* a thing. If we are all great, wise and all knowing, what could we possibly learn? Nothing. How can you learn something that you already know? We are here to *experience* what we already know. And, at some point in the journey, we will all awaken and remember *who we really are* - whether it is in this life or another one. In the meantime, let us approach the journey of our lives, with a sense of fun and adventure, knowing that one day we will wake up and remember that this is what we intended in the first place.

Look back at your life objectively. What pattern, of lower vibration emotion, has played itself over and over again: anger, jealousy, hate, abandonment, entrapment or sadness? Please describe. What is the opposite of the emotion you have experienced most? (Whatever it is, this is what you have come here to experience.)

What will happen to your life once you experience your true nature?

What problems and issues will fall away?

What would you finally be able to laugh at?

What could you create?

THE WIZARD

If Life is Art, you are the Artist!

There was a great leader and wizard, of a mystical land, who knew how to create all he desired, through his thoughts, feelings and intentions. One day, he went on a walk through his beautiful forest. He experienced the splendid smell of exotic flowers, the playful sound of animals, the vast blueness of the eternal sky and the luxurious moist grass, beneath his bare feet. He was both intoxicated by the experience and amused by it, for he knew that he was *the creator of all that is*. He knew that he created the exotic flowers, the melodic birds, the eternal sky and the wild grass below his bare feet, simply with the *magic of his mind*. He rejoiced in his creations, as he continued to walk.

In his intoxication (he must have been having an out of body experience), he fell and hit his head. When he awoke just minutes later, he couldn't remember anything of his life before, or his magical powers. Suddenly, he was experiencing himself, to be alone in a very scary forest. The birds sounded like wild hawks, ready to attack, the sky looked ominous, and without shoes, he was subject to all sorts of dangers. Without remembering who he was, he experienced himself as frightened and powerless. Instead of acting fearlessly, as the creator of all around him, he began to make up stories about himself and his life – just like all humans do, who don't remember their own magic and power. Stories that made him feel weak and vulnerable.

Trying to make meaning out of his experience, he told himself that someone must have beaten him up, and dragged him to the forest, to die. Why else would he have a huge painful bump on his head, and be barefoot in the dangerous forest? Maybe, this person was watching him now, and was ready to pounce on him, at any moment? He could feel fear pulse through his body. He got up and began to move, but as he did, he heard wild animals in the forest, and he was certain that they wanted to kill him, as well. He knew he had to defend himself so he made a spear. He would kill them first. And that is exactly what he did. He spent the rest of his life, in the unforgiving forest, simply trying to survive, by killing anything that seemed to pose a threat. He lived his entire life just trying to survive, and never again enjoying the life that he himself could not remember creating.

For years, the town's people looked for him, but could not find him. He had learned to be a good warrior and hid well when he perceived himself to be hunted. One day, when he was dying, one of the town's people stumbled across his weary body. The townsman almost didn't recognize the wizard because his appearance had changed so drastically. The townsman bent down to the wizard to offer him help, but the wizard glared back with fear and distrust. The townsman tried to remind the wizard of who he was, and that *he was the creator of all he experienced*. Although the wizard felt something familiar (like a dream) in the man's words, the wizard was too caught up in 30 years of his own story to remember.

When the wizard died that day and awoke from his story in the after-life, he clearly saw that, in his ignorance, to uncover the truth of who he was, he invented a convincing story about life. Once he created the story, he spent the rest of his life proving it was true. He laughed when he realized that even in his seeming powerlessness he had still created all around him. He saw that as his story became one of survival and fear, the forest actually changed to make his story true. The animals did, in fact, become vicious, the plants poisonous and real dangers lurked at every turn. Whether the wizard remembered his powers or not, he was still creating everything around him. He was still a great powerful spiritual being, whether he knew himself to be so or not.

Most of us are living in a state of amnesia and forgetting that we are also a great powerful wizard. Instead of reclaiming and honoring our power, as the creators of our lives, we are making up stories of powerlessness and fear, and as a result, creating a life that proves our stories true. But, like the wizard, we are still creating all around us – we are just not doing it consciously or with conscious intention.

You can't stop being a spiritual creator no matter what you do. You are constantly creating the life you live and all you perceive to be true. You can choose to create consciously, or you can keep telling yourself stories of powerlessness and as a result, keep manifesting a reality to support your stories.

Is it time to wake up from your false stories? How do you know it is a false story? Simple - it makes you feel bad. The truth, of who you really are, will never ever make you feel anything less than a great, powerful, loving being.

No matter what, one day, you too will awaken. But until you do, like the wizard, you can't change the essence of who you really are.

Wake up my dear friend – the adventure of your precious life awaits.

Waking Up

When you remove all illusion, Joy is your natural state of being!

No one ever judged the sleeping wizard, for even in his amnesia, he was still the wizard. No one is judging you for your amnesia, or me for mine. And, there is no reason to judge yourself; in fact, the judgment keeps you drugged and invested in your stories. If you want to begin to wake up - either because you know it is time, or your story has become too painful - simply start questioning your story. Start asking yourself "Where did my story begin?" And, "How do I know it is true?" And finally, create a new story which supports a higher version of the life you really want to create.

Spiritual Myth -
Self judgment makes us better people and keeps us on our path.

The human mind has a need to make sense of everything. It is part of how we survive. By giving things meaning, it gives us a sense of security and that enables us to function in the world – even if that meaning makes us feel like helpless little children. The problem, with the stories we tell ourselves, is that we start telling them before we can even walk and talk. Babies start defining their worlds, by the stories they make up about everything around them. They decide whether it is safe or scary; whether they are lovable or unlovable; and whether they can take chances or must protect themselves.

Our personalities are defined before the age of five, because we already have enough stories in place, to have a sense of certainty and knowingness about life and who we think we are. Then, we spend the rest of our lives proving that our stories are true. That's not hard to do because, unless challenged, the mind will select only information that supports our stories. But, even more importantly, the universe constantly reorganizes itself to make our stories right. Our stories, which are our collective thoughts, create exactly what we experience. Every time we give energy to a story (add to our collective thoughts), we are sending out energy that re-organizes or reinforces the energy that makes up our reality – all that we know and experience. In other words, thoughts, feelings and intentions are the fabrics of creating the lives we experience, and we are no more victims of circumstance or karma than

our bodies are victims to unhealthy elements that we ingest.

There's nothing wrong with creating life through the stories we tell – it's all just part of the grand adventure. The problem is we have forgotten that we are the story tellers and creators of what we call reality, and, as a result, we experience tons of pain. That, in itself, is another grand spiritual adventure, but for many of us, we are tired of that same old painful adventure, and we are ready to experience adventures of joy, peace and love.

In order to experience that new adventure, we need a new story - a story that supports joy, peace and love. But, even more difficult than creating a new story, is giving up the old one. When we have decades invested in that old story, it's hard to give it up. It's what has shaped our personality, identity and knowing of ourselves. It has created a sense of human security, and it is all we know. Giving up the story means giving up a part of ourselves, and it can be scary and overwhelming.

You can't give up the story overnight but, you can start questioning the story. As you pick at it, little by little, the story, like a scab over a healed cut, will fall away to reveal new flesh and a new life. You and the power of who you really are still exist under your story. Not even the best or most painful story in the world can destroy the truth of who you really are.

What has been the story of your life?

Create a new story for your life that supports Joy, Peace and Love:

REMEMBER

Poor behavior is not a sign of inadequate spirituality but rather a sign of fearful story telling.

It is only the stories we tell ourselves that make us act in ways that seem less than spiritual. If you remembered your power, and who you really are, as God energy, and that you created your world and could re-create it at will, would you ever be angry, frustrated, jealous or scared? No. You would, in fact, only experience the loving nature of who you really are. We only act in these "unspiritual" ways because we have forgotten the truth of our eternal natures.

It's time to Remember...

There is no reason to be hard on yourself when your humanness takes over and makes you act – human. In your imperfection – you are perfect.

It's time to start honoring yourself, above all, and loving yourself unconditionally – warts and all. When you know total and absolute self-love, no matter how much you may screw up or, even blow up – a strange and magical thing happens – you'll find a joy and peace so deep that, no matter where your adventure takes you, or you take your adventure, you'll never be alone or fearful. You'll know the fullness of your life that you, as God, intended it to be.

DIRTY LAUNDRY....

When you release your made up meanings of how things should be and how people should act, the real meaning of life begins to emerge, and you are swept away with the beauty and wonderment all around you.

Do you believe that you have to do something or attain something, in order to experience joy? What if that wasn't true and joy was the natural essence of who you really are and it was available to you every moment of your life?

If joy is present in our being, all the time, why don't we experience it more? Could it be that we are so busy chasing after it that, the very chase keeps us from it? If we believe that something must happen in our lives, in order to feel joy, we will forever be searching – whether that something is a relationship, money, status, or, even retirement. You can't chase after something that you already have within your being, and, in fact, the search outside yourself distracts you from what already exists, just by being *who you really are*.

By outwardly looking for joy, not only do we overlook what already exists as our true natures, but also, we often end up with feelings of inadequacy, disappointment, jealousy (if someone else has what we want), and even anger, when we fail to attain the thing that we think might finally bring us the joy we frantically desire. We might even experience feelings of undeserving and unworthiness. But, how can we be undeserving of experiencing the breath and life force of *who we really are*? Often, when we give up the endless search for joy, and we unlock ourselves from all that entraps us in the futile search, *it* finds us.

Spiritual Myth -
Suffering brings us closer to God

Years ago, I lost my favorite sweater. I searched all over the house for it, asked my whole family if they saw it, looked in the dog's stash of stolen items, and even started to wonder if it ever even existed. Finally, after hours of not finding it, I gave up. It wasn't until days later, when I was catching up on wash that I found it buried in the bottom of the laundry basket, under my dirty laundry. It had been there all along, but I never thought to look there because, I was distracted looking for it in the places I imagined it might be. It wasn't until I gave up the search, and got on

with my life, that what I was looking for, found me. Could it be that the joy you are seeking is also buried beneath your "dirty laundry" – waiting patiently to be uncovered?

Your dirty laundry is your disappointment, your expectations, your jealousy, your anger, your regret, your anxiety and your fear. Every time you tell yourself a story and make up a meaning that leaves you disappointed, jealous, angry, anxious or fearful, you add another piece of dirty laundry – ultimately covering up your joy. Most of the dirty laundry you create occurs in the search for finding what you are looking for, in the world, rather than within yourself.

Joy, however, remains untouched, and intact, no matter what you throw on top of it. It is the core of who you are. If you want to experience your true nature of joy, all you have to do is stop creating more dirty laundry, and start cleaning up yesterday's dirty laundry. As it gets rung out in the spin cycle, you'll discover that joy is ever present, and there is nothing more you need to do.

When you release your *made up meanings* of how things should be and how people should act, the real meaning of life begins to emerge, and you are swept away with the beauty and wonderment all around you. When your *made-up meaning* is removed from the events that happen in your life, your story will begin to dissolve. And, as your story dissolves, you will become more present with the moment. Then something amazing happens; a new joyful meaning overcomes you. Like a flower blossoming in the spring, you overflow with presence, and joy floods your mind, body and soul. You have returned home to your true nature.

Describe the "dirty laundry"
that has hidden your joy:

____

____

____

____

____

____

____

____

____

DISSOLVING THE STORY

Change your mind – Change your life

Most stories don't dissolve overnight, and many take years to dissolve. Dissolving a story can be like picking a scab; if you pick it before the wound is healed, the scab will grow back and scarring could result. Your story has served a purpose because it has helped you survive and get through life. It has also helped you evolve to the point where you now recognize that you might not need the story anymore, and there is a grand life to create beyond the story.

When my oldest son was about 8 years old, I slipped an "I love you" note into his lunch box. When he came home later that day, he was unusually happy. When I asked him how his day went, he told me that a girl loves him – he didn't know who it was, but he found her *love note* in his lunch box. I held my secret for 10 years, because this story made him feel so good about himself, added a sense of wonderment to his life, and he felt lovable. There was no reason for me to take the story away from him. For all those years, he had no idea it wasn't true. When I eventually did tell him, we both laughed about it – because the story no longer mattered. When we finally feel good about who we are, we can dissolve any story without harming ourselves, or tearing our identity apart. From a place of unconditional self-love, it is possible to dissolve any story.

There are four types of disempowering stories: victimhood, powerlessness, loss and unworthiness. The following is designed to help you start questioning and understanding your own stories. I suggest approaching your life stories with a sense of humor, curiosity and acceptance.

Meg grew up in a middle class family. She was the oldest of four children. Since her mother was sick on a regular basis and her father traveled for work, she became the family's care-taker. By the time she grew up, her primary life story was "I have to take care of everyone. There is nothing left for me. I have to be strong and hide my own needs." As an adult, she had 2 children and her

husband left her, with no emotional or financial support, for another woman. Meg was "forced" to work two jobs, and be the primary care-taker for her children and her now invalid mother. She was never able to pursue her dreams, and she over-looked her own needs, until she herself became sick. The meaning Meg gave to the events in her life kept her trapped in a perpetual story of victimhood and powerlessness.

How can we be certain that the meaning she gave her life is really true? Yes, she has been the primary caretaker throughout her whole life, but why does it mean that "she has to take care of everyone but herself"? It doesn't. What if Meg started telling herself a story that makes her feel powerful? It could be something like this; "I am strong, smart and independent, and I can easily take care of myself as well as I have taken care of everyone else. My needs are just as important as everyone else's". What type of life experiences do you think might show up with this new story line? Anything is possible – maybe Meg will start pursuing her own dreams; maybe she'll attract a supportive and loyal mate; maybe, her mother would even become more self-sufficient. Because life will unconditionally support our stories, anything and everything is possible.

Dan grew up in New York City and lived with his grandmother until he was 15 years old, and she died suddenly of a heart attack. His mother abandoned him shortly after birth, and she never revealed his father's identity. From the age of 15 to 23, Dan lived off the streets and never trusted anyone. He believed that he wasn't worthy of love, and if anyone got too close, they too would leave him. His primary story was one of loss and unworthiness.

What would happen if Dan stopped giving negative meaning to the events in his life? What if he just observed the events in his life, without putting any judgments on them? Yes, his mother left him, he never knew his father, and his grandmother and only caretaker died when he was still very young. Where does that say he was unlovable or everyone is going to leave him? Can you prove that meaning is true? No, of course not. It's only true in Dan's mind. And, because he believes it is true, he gives energy to it, and as a result, attracts more of the same. If Dan could change his story and what he believed to be true, his whole life would change to support him.

Ellie was raised in a traditional, middle-class home with two parents, who grew up during

the depression. Her parents carefully taught her about scarcity, and that she had to save or there wouldn't be enough. As a result, Ellie learned to do without. While all the other kids were out riding their bikes, or going on summer vacations, Ellie told herself stories that she didn't deserve what seemed to come to other kids more easily. As an adult, Ellie has settled for less than rewarding relationships, and a job she can't stand. Living out a story-line of unworthiness, she never pursued her love of art, or her dream of buying a home.

How might Ellie's life turn out differently, if she told herself a different story? Is it Ellie's childhood experiences that created her stories, or her interpretation of them? What would happen to Ellie's story, if she started to really love and value herself? If she unconditionally loved and valued herself, could she continue to identify with a story of unworthiness? With a new story of deserving, what might she attract and create?

It is not what happens to you in your life - it is the stories that you make up about what happens that makes you feel as you do, and manifests a life that supports your stories. This is how powerful you are. Your story is compelling and true, only because you make it so with your thoughts and emotions. You have the free will to change your story at any time, and once committed to your new empowering story, you will experience the powerful manifestation of a new life – this is universal law. The manifestation of your life can be no more or less than the thoughts you think and the stories you believe.

Change your mind - Change your life.

Write a 5 page autobiography of your life. Start at your childhood and work your way to the present time. Include whatever you can remember - like thoughts, feelings and the interpretations you made. Once you complete it, go back and read it. Objectively, look for patterns or recurring stories or themes. Write it all down. You might also ask a good friend to help you with this. Once complete, answer the following questions.

What stories have created your life, in the past and present?

Are your stories the result of victimhood, powerlessness, unworthiness or loss? Give examples:

When you look at your stories impartially, what arguments can you make against your stories to prove them untrue?

Is it possible to give up these stories?

What would happen to your stories, right now, if you unconditionally loved yourself?

How might your life change without these stories attached to it?

Write a new story which supports the life you really desire.

Jesus Rejoiced on The Cross?

There are no negative experiences – only the stories we make up about them.

There are no bad or negative experiences. What makes them seem bad or negative is the meaning we put on them – the stories that we make up about them. Two people can have the same exact life experience, and one person puts a negative meaning on it, and experiences grief, and the other uses it to empower his life and experiences great abundance.

There is a story of two brothers. They were the sons of, what most people would call, an evil man. The father of these sons was imprisoned for rape, murder, and a lot of other heinous crimes. One son turned out just like him, and spent his whole life either committing crimes, or being punished for them. The other son became a successful member of the community, contributed to many, and had a beautiful, happy family. The first son was interviewed and asked "Why do you think you turned out like you did?" His response was "with a father like that, how could I have turned out any other way?" When the second, successful son was asked the same question, his response was "with a father like that, how could I have turned out any other way?"

Which "brother" do you choose to be? Every moment of your life, you are making this choice.

Your life, and the joy you feel and express in your life, are no less or greater than the meaning you give to your life experiences. It is not what happens in your life; it is how you mentally and emotionally define your experiences.

Jesus was crucified by people who feared and hated him, and because he was an awakened being, I bet he didn't put a negative meaning on it. If we could have read his mind, he might have thought "poor souls – you don't remember who you are because, if you did, you wouldn't need to do this" or, he might have thought "my crucifixion will make my message go down in history – I wondered how I would make that happen – wow, that was easier than I thought it would be". The more awake and aware we are, the more we can reject the stories that others tell us, and even the disempowering ones we tell ourselves. We can then begin to shake out the illusion of truth, until we are left with a greater knowing, that we are beyond all the made-up truths that have tugged on us for lifetimes. No matter how real you think your life experiences are, your life is no more or less than the stories you continue to tell yourself, day after day.

Our experiences completely depend on the meanings that we give them.

It is not our experiences that cause us pain; it is our mental interpretation of the experiences – the meaning we put on them. That meaning is derived from a life full of prior and current experiences. We all have the ability to change or alter our interpretation, at any time - to change the meaning. All meanings you put on an experience will serve you in creating your life but some will support a more desirable life than others. Meanings change, when either they no longer serve you, or you experience so much pain, that you start seeking another meaning.

You are the creator of your reality, and nothing can hurt you unless you believe it into being so. The world is at your command, and you get to create the life you truly want, simply by the thoughts you think and the energy you put into them.

What meaning do you give to the most challenging situation in your life?

____

____

____

____

What meaning would empower you to, either rise above the situation, or for you to have a completely different approach?

____

____

____

____

____

The Meaningless Life

Happy people tell themselves happy stories...
Sad people tell themselves sad stories...
Spiritually awakened people don't tell themselves any stories...

When I was seventeen years old, I found myself unexpectedly pregnant. In my shock and disbelief, I walked around aimlessly, for two weeks telling myself that my life was over. I had big plans of traveling around the world, and a baby, especially at the age of seventeen, didn't fit into that plan. The meaning I gave to this unexpected pregnancy was of doom and gloom. It's almost 27 years later and I have to honestly say that the meaning I made up during those two weeks of shock was completely wrong. I did have the baby, and I did put my traveling plans on hold, for a while, but having my son didn't end my life, it enriched my life beyond anything I could have dreamed possible. I can't imagine what I would have missed if I had made a different decision. He has been the light of my life, and even now,he is my best friend, business partner, adventure buddy, and one of the most extraordinary people I have ever known.

If I am really honest, virtually all the negative meanings I have assigned to situations in my life were wrong too. Even things that seemed horrific, at the time, somehow turned out well – either leading to an opportunity, saving me from a mistake, or creating an epiphany that changed my life. Knowing this, I am not so quick to give worrisome meaning to the things in my life. It is especially on those days, when I am completely present in my body, and aware of my feelings that I can choose to make the events in my life "meaningless". When I am just present with whatever happens, without deciding if it is good or bad, I find peace and clarity, and really enjoy the experiences of my life.

It's not an easy task to remove disempowering stories from our lives. After all, we have automatically been putting meaning on every moment of our lives, since birth. But where has it led us? Most of the time, the meanings that we give to life make us fearful, anxious and distrustful, and we never really know the truth of the situation. We particularly do this in

relationships. When someone's behavior doesn't seem in alignment with how we think they should act, we often take it personally – maybe even deciding that they don't love us anymore. When, in fact, the truth is that they are just having a bad day, or their own stories are affecting how they respond in the world. When they see us react, they too put meaning on our behavior, and react to that. A never-ending, vicious cycle is created by the use of made-up meaning.

Our innate wisdom is expressed when we realize that we don't know the true meaning of life's events. It's quite possible that something, which seems awful, turns out to be a blessing in disguise, and maybe, even leads us to what we really want.

There was a farmer who owned just one horse. One day, his horse ran away and all the town's people said "Oh, poor farmer Joe, his only horse ran away – how will he be able to plow his land – isn't it terrible!" When farmer Joe heard what the people said, he responded "Maybe – maybe not". A few days later, his horse came back and brought another horse with him. All the town's people declared "Farmer Joe is the luckiest man in town – now he has two horses – he is so lucky!" Farmer Joe responded "Maybe – maybe not". The new horse needed to be broken in, so Farmer Joe's only son went out to do the job. But, the new horse was too wild and threw the son. The son ended up with a major leg fracture. The whole town declared "Poor Farmer Joe, his only son has broken his leg – who will tend the land? It's so terrible!" Farmer Joe responded "Maybe – maybe not". A couple of weeks later, war broke out and all the young men in town were called to fight and soon died; all except Farmer Joe's son, who had a broken leg, and couldn't go off to war.

Maybe – Maybe not.
Author Unknown.

As soon as we give anything meaning, we identify with it, and when the thing we give meaning to changes, we are emotionally affected by those changes, as well. When how we feel at any given moment is contingent on the events in our lives, we become the emotional slaves of external events. One day we might feel great, but the next could be awful. When we remove meaning from our lives, we begin to flow with life, and are totally unaffected emotionally by what does or doesn't happen. We live in a state of faith that opens us up to unconditional inner peace and joy.

Can you imagine how much more relaxed and joyful you would be everyday, if you stopped putting your made-up, human meanings on everything? The truth is that we don't really know the meaning of anything, because we don't see the big picture. When we are wise enough to recognize and accept our limited perceptions, and we can trust a greater force, we begin to merge with our God-center, and our lives unfold, as beautiful, magical dances, which always support our highest good.

Describe a life experience that seemed to be horrible at the time, but somehow, turned out to be a blessing in disguise:

How would you feel, if you knew that everything that happens in your life is really supporting your highest good?

How might a current, challenging situation be supportive of your highest good?

Mind Mastering

Freedom is the end result of mastering your own mind!

Joyful living is always available to us, if we have the courage, strength and devotion to relinquish our made-up meanings of life events, and the unrealistic criteria for what we think makes us happy. It's simple, but not at all easy. The only true cause of unhappiness is being the victims of our thoughts and servants of our minds. The greatest and only imprisonment comes when we are mastered *by* our minds, and led to believe that we are trapped within the creation of our stories. True freedom happens when we realize that the key to changing our lives is changing our thoughts – to become the masters of our own minds. Could it be that this is our only real challenge, and the secret to unleashing all that is possible?

Mastering your mind means becoming conscious of all your thoughts. As you become conscious of your thoughts, you do not judge them, give power to them or identify with them. In other words, you do not even give meaning to your thoughts. You let them flow by, as if you are merely an observer and not even the owner of them. As you stop giving meaning to your thoughts and the events in your life, the events that used to cause you pain, will also begin to dissolve. Your thoughts and feelings will no longer be giving energy to events and holding them in physical form with your attention.

I'm not saying that you should go around affirming that everything is meaningless - just the opposite. Everything is meaningful. What I am saying is that the meaning you are giving life events is not working for you if you are not experiencing joy and peace every day of your life, and that your life is incongruent with what you really want.

When we remove "made-up meaning", we can begin to see things for what they truly are, and we can begin to feel the beauty and love of those around us. We begin to see past the mask of illusion and discover that what lies beneath that illusion is an ingenious world of incredible manifestation; a world waiting to provide us with our every desire, simply by the magic of our pure loving thoughts.

On a scale of one to ten, how much joy do you experience on most days?

____

____

____

What story most affects your ability to feel joy?

____

____

____

____

____

____

____

____

____

____

____

What would happen if your story dissolved, or was replaced with a new happier story?

Mental Supervision

True spiritual freedom comes when we stop giving life meaning and we allow life to give us meaning.

Would you allow a five-year-old to play unsupervised in the street? Of course not; but this is exactly what we do when we allow our thoughts to run rampant, without supervision. Our minds are always looking for something to be anxious over. It's almost as if there are little police officers in our heads looking for problems to worry about. As soon as one problem is resolved, those little guys will find another. No wonder so many of us are on Prozac or not able to sleep at night. Of course, the purpose of these guys is to protect us from danger, and to do so they must be on guard for potential problems. But, it never ends – whether or not there is really something to be worried about. The real problem is that if we are always anxious and worrying about something, we never get to relax and be present in the moment – which is where peace and joy are waiting.

These mind police are on the outlook for the meanings we put on events and experiences in our lives. They don't create the meaning – they simply react to the meaning we invent. As soon as we invent a potentially dangerous meaning, they react and make us feel anxious. If we interpret our lover's lack of calling as abandonment, they are on guard. If there is not enough money in our bank accounts and we think we are going to be evicted, they come to attention. If our child is sick, and we imagine the worst, they give us enough anxiety to keep us up all night. They are good at what they do, but they are only servants of our minds, and they are triggered by the meanings we give our experiences.

The way to keep the mind police at bay is mental supervision. We need to supervise our thoughts and the meaning we give to everything around us. Instead of believing everything we think, we allow our thoughts to slide on by, without identifying with them, as if they were a dream. We become so aware of our feelings that as soon as we find ourselves feeling bad, we immediately know it is because of the meaning

we have put on something. When we remove the meaning, suddenly we feel better and move back into alignment with *who we really are*. It is then, and only then, that we can begin to discover the real magical meaning of life.

Make a list of all the thoughts that cause you feelings of fear, worry, anxiety or, any other unwanted feelings:

What is true and untrue about these thoughts?

What thoughts do you want to supervise, and not give energy to in the future?

...Just As You Are

It is through the experience of our present moment that we expand in our greatness.

It is in our nature to want to grow and experience ourselves as *even more*. This intrinsic desire allows us to expand into the greatness of who we really are. The problem is when we deny our current experience and painfully judge ourselves. Every time we judge ourselves, we are really resisting our humanness and this separates us from our divinity. Any judgment, or resistance to our experience, keeps us from integrating our human selves with our spiritual selves and actually keeps us from the growth we seek.

Judgment keeps us from experiencing our present moment, yet it is through the experience of our present moment that we expand in our greatness.

No matter what you are experiencing in your life, and how it makes you feel, you are so much greater than anything you humanly perceive. By remembering this, it can empower you to stay present with whatever experience is happening in the outside world and even your response to it. When you remember and embrace the power and spiritual essence of who you really are, without denying yourself in any way, you move into the center of your experience, without falling victim to a story, or losing your self in the humanness of feeling.

It is only possible to truly be present in any experience, when we already know that we are greater than what we are experiencing or perceiving. We must remember that we are not our feelings or thoughts.

Spiritual myth -
we must rise above our humanness.

We can easily accept and appreciate our humanness when we no longer identify with it or make it larger than us. When we accept and even appreciate our humanness, despite our flaws, faults and less than ideal reactions to undesirable situations, we are thrown back into our own spiritual center, and we are reunited with who we really are.

There is a dance that happens along the spiritual path. It is like a dance of a new day's light, piercing through a paned window. It doesn't stay still, for, in its essence, it must keep moving. Like the sun's light upon the earth, you too must keep moving. It is your essence. Even when you surpass your human entrapments of false identity and made up stories, you will continue to move more and more - towards your spiritual center. For in movement, you are centered.

Even now, in our human form, in movement we become more and more centered. The movement happens when we stop identifying with who we think we are, our stories and even our feelings. When we release this identification, we actually become more connected to our experiences and the movement of our feelings. Instead of pulling us down and becoming stagnant in an old story or feeling, we experience it in a whole new light. We discover a new dance of embracing our humanness with curiosity and wonder. When we become present with experience and feelings, we immediately move into the center of knowing ourselves and experiencing the spiritual eternal essence of who we really are.

This dance of movement, from humanity into spiritual light, can only happen when we stop judging our experience and resisting what is. When we approach our life with a sense of loving acceptance, movement happens and what once was stagnated is now released.

Discovering our spiritual center does not happen as a result of denying or undermining our humanness. It happens when we love and embrace every aspect of who we are, and the mystery of our lives. It happens when we can laugh at ourselves, and know that there are greater forces at work, even if we can't see them or understand them.

The path to our spiritual center is right through the humanness of our experience, and the secret, to making it there, is the courage to be present and conscious without judgment or resistance.

What experiences are you now resisting or judging?

What would happen if you approached these experiences with a sense of wonder, and became completely present, without any sense of judgment or resistance?

Finding Your *Self* in Chaos!

Bad behavior doesn't mean that we are not spiritual; it just means that we are pushed to our emotional limits, because our wounds are being triggered.

We've all had those days when everything seems to go wrong; the car breaks down, the dog bites the kid next door, someone drives through your fence and you discover that the strange knocking in your living room is a family of woodpeckers having babies in the walls (based on my true life experiences). You might think, how can anyone be spiritual when life just doesn't give you a break? And then when we do react in less than desirable ways, we judge ourselves for being stressed, angry or just plain mean.

First, I want to tell you that there is no higher being judging you or wishing that you react any other way than how you are. God loves you unconditionally, and doesn't expect anything –

ever. I'm not saying that there might not be a better way to respond in chaos or crisis, but it's all perfect. It always is and always will be. You are a Godly being having a human adventure. After this adventure is done, you'll still be a Godly being and you might choose to have another similar adventure in another lifetime – maybe, to see if you can respond more in a way that is in integrity with who you really are. Life is not a game you win at – there is no winning or losing, and believe it or not, there is no good or bad. No matter what everyone has told you, there is no judge or jury, and there is no right way *to do* your life.

Having said all that, our souls have an innate pull to be in alignment with the highest good of all. Spiritual Alignment results in living a life of peace, love and joy. When we deviate from this spiritual center, we just don't feel good. That's why our negative reactions make us feel crappy. It's these uncomfortable feelings that let us know we are out of alignment, and it's a message that we can use to shift our understanding, awareness and/or behavior so that we can return to our center of love, peace and joy. Life is a journey of moving away from one's center; experiencing emotional discomfort, and then finding a road back - through a new insight, awareness, or shift

in consciousness - ultimately effecting the choices we make and the way we act in the world.

It is never really a situation that disturbs us – even when it seems that way. It's the meaning we give it, and the way in which we react to it that causes us pain.

Challenging situations are put in place by our own manifestation. Unconsciously, we create these challenging situations because our thoughts, feelings and beliefs attract them. Our reactions to the challenges are then clues to our unhealed wounds – our negative stories. As long as a wound remains open, and an unhealthy story is never questioned, the universe will generously bring to you the manifestation of the story or wound so that you can experience the (often unconscious) story in the physical world. It's a gift! And, it is how the universe works.

Once the challenge or situation is present in your life, and you react in a way that makes you feel bad, those bad feelings will make you look inside yourself, to find a way to feel better. Until we are devoted to that spiritual journey, we might turn to food, alcohol, drugs, TV or any other distraction or addiction, to feel better. But, every time we do, we miss the opportunity to shift a belief, change a story or discover something about ourselves that might help us. Those bad feelings are a signal that your story is not in alignment with your highest good, and they create an opportunity to grow and discover a greater you. By the way, what is in your highest good is always in everyone's highest good. This is a universal law.

Here's what it can look like:

- *You have a negative story.*
- *It manifests as a challenging situation.*
- *You have a negative reaction.*
- *You feel bad about your reaction.*
- *You look inside to feel better.*
- *You discover an old wound or story playing out.*
- *You take the opportunity to heal it – ultimately moving back toward your own center of love, joy and peace.*

Bad behavior doesn't mean that we are not spiritual; it just means that we are pushed to our emotional limits, because our wounds are being

triggered. Responding in a spiritual way means that we use the situation as an opportunity to learn something about ourselves, get in touch with the story that made us react as we did and to question the story until it starts to lose its power and eventually dissolve.

How do you know it's a story? It's all a story. Life is a story we make up – that's how the energy is held in place and we have a world to live in. The question is not "is there a story?" There is. The question is "is the story one that supports feeling good or one that supports feeling bad?" People, who are happy and joyful, have stories that support happy and joyful experiences. People, who are miserable, have stories that support pain. It is as simple as that. Change your story – change your life.

A few years ago, I walked in on my son, Travis, who was about 7 years old at the time. He was uncontrollably crying. I asked him what was making him cry so hard – he responded beneath his crying hysteria by saying "Clay took my toy!!!!" Clay, his younger brother, by two years, was nowhere to be seen, and there was a toy in Travis's hand. I looked at the toy and said "That toy?" Another barely plausible

"Yes!!!!" came out of Travis. He had somehow gotten the toy back from his younger brother, but he was still telling himself a story about losing it. I thought for a second, and without warning I said, "Travis, remember when we went to Disneyland, and we went on all the rides and you got to meet Mickey Mouse?" As I went on about Disneyland Travis started to laugh and smile. Then I said "Oh, but Clay took your toy". Travis started to cry uncontrollably, once again. Then I quickly said something else about Disneyland, and Travis started to laugh. But, then I reminded him that Clay took his toy and he started to cry. We went through about seven rounds of this, until Travis stopped reacting to either story, because he realized what was happening. When he told himself a "poor me" story about losing something he loved, he felt bad, but as soon as he thought of a happy story, he felt happy (notice that neither story had anything to do with what was happening in the moment). It really is that simple.

Travis is 12 years old now and can recognize his own stories. Sometimes he chooses to hold on to them, and sometimes he lets them go, but the best thing of all is that he can choose. A few weeks ago, he was feeling bad about something, and he said to me "I know it's just a story I am telling

myself, but I'm going to choose to believe it, for a little while". "Okay," I said, as I gave him a hug. Sometimes, we just need to experience a certain feeling for a little while, but when we know it is caused by a story, when we are done with the experience, we can let go of the story. If we don't know that it is a story we are telling ourselves, we often get stuck in it and the resulting feelings.

Do you know what your story is? Your life is demonstrating your story to you every day, without fail. The percentage of joy in your life is the percentage of joy in your story. The percentage of sadness in your life is the percentage of sadness in your story. If you are a victim in your life – then, you must be a victim in your story. Are you wealthy in your life? Then, you must be wealthy in your story. The problem is that most of our stories are created by us on an unconscious level – much like our night-time dreams. The trick is to become conscious of the story. Since our lives demonstrate our stories to us, we have all the information we need every day. Each time you have one of those bad feelings or undesirable reactions, it's a clue that your current story doesn't support a life of joy, peace and love. When you go to the movies, you know that the movie was first created by a story-line. Your life is no different. Your life, too, is created by a story-line. You are the writer, actor and producer. If you want to change your life, you must start by changing your story.

Think of a current situation in your life that is causing you pain. Pretend you are the writer of this movie. What is the story-line?

____

____

____

____

How does this story-line support your past experiences?

____

____

____

____

Write a new story which supports joy, peace and love. Remember, you are the writer so, no story is impossible.

FINDING PEACE IN CHAOS

Peace is a result of the stories we tell about our lives, and the meaning we give events – it's that simple.

It is said that the only constant and predictable thing in life is change. Yet, we struggle to keep things the way we know them – thinking that will bring us peace. It often seems that we are either experiencing constant change or chasing the illusive idea of peace - occasionally finding brief moments of peaceful bliss, only to have the next crisis destroy peace once again.

Our journey, in this lifetime, is not to bounce back and forth between peace and change, or even choose one above the other, but rather to discover and experience peace within change and even within chaos.

Peace is nothing more than a mental interpretation of perceived safety. If you can find a place of inner safety, you will forever experience peace. But, if peace is dependent upon external stability and predictability, it will be a distant and long- lost friend. In other words, when your life is free of turmoil, change, crisis, and everyone leaves you alone, only then can you feel peaceful. I believe that allows for about one hour every 50 years in the average, modern day life. If experiencing peace is contingent upon the external world cooperating, that doesn't allow for much opportunity to experience peace.

How do we find peace in a chaotic world?

First, we need to stop thinking that inner peace is a result of outer peace (a calm and non-demanding environment, for example). Inner peace is not dependent on anything external. It is only dependent on you and your interpretations of the world. What you tell yourself about the world and your environment will make the difference between experiencing peace or stress.

Peace is a result of the stories we tell about our lives, and the meaning we give events – it's that simple.

Peace is particularly affected by the degree of faith that we have. If we believe we have to do everything ourselves, and we are all alone to

fail or survive in this great big universe, we will experience enormous amounts of stress. But, if we believe that we are supported and protected by some great loving force, then we can begin to relax quite a bit, and not feel as if we have to be on top of everything.

When we can ride on the wings of the great unknown, and relax in our faith and a greater understanding of who we really are, we can then truly experience the exciting adventure our lives are meant to be. We become the explorers of a whole new world, known only to a few, but available to all.

Spiritual Myth -
Peace is boring

Peace does not create a boring life – it creates the space for unlimited adventure and exploration of great possibilities. When we discover the center of peace, within our own beings, life takes on a whole new meaning. We can participate fully in the journey, because we are no longer afraid of unforeseen consequences or even regrets. We trust the process because we know that somehow we are being guided by our inner wisdom, and protected by the highest power. And, no matter where the road takes us, we will be safe, in the arms of the greatest love.

The experience of peace is not a result, consequence or reward from the outside world. In fact, it has nothing to do with the outside world. The peace we may have spent our lives frantically seeking is inside us - waiting quietly for us, all the time. All we needed to do was to stop taking life so seriously, have faith in a greater power and love and value ourselves a million times more than we thought was possible.

The essence of peace and love is who you really are. It's time to stop covering it up with stories of fear. It's time to embrace the greatness within you and start really living your life according to your grandest dreams. Does that sound boring to you?

What is the thing, situation or person which seems to rob the most peace from you?

What internal shift can you make, in relationship to this thing, situation or person, which would bring you back to peace?

This Moment Only

The key to finding your way back to the moment is to release all judgment and simply observe.

Our most challenging experiences offer us the greatest opportunities to move deeper into our spiritual center, but we also don't have to wait for a crisis or chaos to remind us of who we are. We can reach spiritual peaks, simply by becoming present in this moment. Many of us think we are present, but we are really distracted. Being present means being fully conscious of everything that you are feeling – including the environment around you, and the energy that is created between you and the environment. It means surrendering all judgments, stories and expectations and just sitting in a space of wonderment and curiosity. There is nothing to do or change. You recognize the moment for the perfection that it is.

For many of us, being in nature brings us back into the present moment. When we are away from everything and walking down the beach or through the mountains, we suddenly find that peaceful place inside. It seems that the environmental experience throws us back into our center. But, it is not just the environment. If it were, that would mean that every time we go into nature, we would have the same experience, but it doesn't work like that. If our mental or emotional state is absent from the experience – preoccupied with something else, no matter how breathtaking nature may be, it will leave us empty inside. After a particularly painful break up, I remember witnessing a magnificent sunset and feeling nothing special. I searched for the spiritual oneness that the sight of a sunset usually brought me, but no matter how hard I searched, it wasn't to be found. Just months before, when I was madly in love, even the site of dead grass seemed miraculous, and I felt one with everything.

So, how can you be in the moment when life is pulling you into the past with regret, or pushing you into the future with worry? Sometimes, it seems impossible, and the only thing that you can do is just ride the wave - having faith that it will naturally take you back to your center. But, maybe the key to finding your way back to the

moment is to release all judgment and simply observe. Whatever you feel - you allow it. You sit in it. You watch it without judging it. And, in an instant, or day, or week, or month, without warning, something changes and you find yourself back *in the moment* – as if you never left.

The path of acceptance brings you back to the moment, but it is love and gratitude that moves you into your center of joy and bliss. We are never more centered in the now then when we are most grateful. You can't be grateful and distracted at the same time. Gratitude throws us into the moment. When we are in awe of a powerful ocean tide, wild flowers on the side of the road or a newborn baby taking her first breath, we are never more present in the now. We feel immense gratitude for what is. The secret to being in the now, every moment, is to find gratitude for life and all adventures – no matter how challenging – remembering that you are the creator of your life, and all that is – and what a wonderful adventure you have created.

List 50 things you are grateful for:

From Chaos to Creation!

Finding your way out of chaos often means experiencing more internal chaos, because you must break down a life that has created the chaos in the first place.

Life is not meant to be painful, yet most of the world would agree, it is. There's no denying that life is filled with ups and downs and sometimes, it seems that there are a lot more downs than there are ups. How do we find and stay in our spiritual center, when the challenges of every day life throw us into perpetual chaos? First of all, there is nothing wrong with experiencing chaos. It's o.k. Even in chaos, your spiritual self stays whole and grows. But, there will come a time in your life that you will become tired of chaos and try to find a way out. Even then, your soul grows. Your chaos might be an out of control life, an unhealthy relationship, an unfulfilling job, health issues, lack of abundance or anything else that causes you pain.

Finding your way out of chaos often means experiencing more internal chaos, because you must break down a life that has created the chaos in the first place. It means that you must question your stories and beliefs, and the way in which you have lived your life, up until now. It means you must take responsibility for everything in your life, without shame, blame or self-judgment. It's not an easy process to shift a lifetime of patterns that have manifested the chaos or unhappiness you might now be experiencing. But, when it is time, there is no turning back. You have reached a level of consciousness that knows there is more to your life than what you have been experiencing, and it's time for that "more". You now welcome a life that can support peace, joy and the certainty of who you really are.

Are you afraid that a peaceful life might be boring, and you are addicted to your chaos? I am not suggesting that you become a monk, and sit on a mountain top, meditating the rest of your life. I am suggesting that, from a peaceful center, you can consciously choose an even grander and more joyful adventure than you ever imagined possible. So, instead of living a life where you must defend against unforeseen challenges and obstacles to survive, you can consciously create all that you want by dreaming a better story and

giving meaning to your life in a way that supports your highest good and grandest desires.

As you begin the journey of finding your way out of chaos, can you acknowledge just how interesting and purposeful your chaos has been? Maybe, your chaos has even gifted you with greater desire and clarity to create a grander and more purposeful life. Describe how your chaos has been purposeful and what direction it has given you:

____

____

____

____

____

____

____

____

____

____

TRUE INSPIRATION

Your greatest challenges can be your greatest gifts.

Getting a grim health report at the doctor's office can make someone take charge of their body. Getting fired can inspire someone to start their own business. Having freedom taken away can make someone fight for the freedom of others. Experiencing trauma can inspire someone to make a difference in the world and discover their life's purpose. My greatest crisis led me to my path and yours can too.

When I was sixteen years old, I unconsciously manifested a violent relationship. It lasted for about a year and during that year, I experienced incredible abuse, at the hands of a boyfriend. Although it took me years to recover, *it scarred me with the intense desire to help* other women and girls uncover their own self-esteem, and get out of violent relationships. By the time I was 25, I was volunteering at crisis centers, domestic abuse hotlines, and safe houses. My desire grew and grew, and I discovered that my life's purpose was to help people discover their own unconditional worth and explore and express their intrinsic power. It went beyond counseling people in crisis to empowering people to discover the power of who they really are. When I list all the most wonderful things I am most grateful for, the nearly deadly abuse I experienced at 16 is right up there on that list. Without it, I might never have found my life's calling, and what my soul came here to do. I am so lucky! The tragedies in our lives don't just make us stronger, by giving us emotional calluses - they have the potential to move us forward on the path of our highest good.

From destruction comes creation. The mountains are created from earthquakes and sometimes majestic and magical islands, like the island of Santorini in Greece, manifest from violent volcanoes. From crisis comes possibility and purpose. It is true for the Earth and it is true for us. There is no crisis in your life that will not leave you without enormous gifts. But, it is your job to see those gifts and use them to create a grander, more purposeful life – whatever that might look like for you.

What crisis in your life has led you to a greater good?

Is it possible that a current challenge also has that potential? How?

What story would you have to give up to discover that potential now rather than later?

Judgment Be Gone!

When you stop judging your own life, you won't be judging anyone else's.

True or false: to be a good, spiritual person, you must never judge anyone? Not so. As humans, we judge everything and everyone. It's in our genetic make up to constantly be making judgments about the world - it is part of our survival mechanism. Our judgments are a gauge for how we make choices and navigate through life, and they are very useful. We automatically make judgments, no matter how well intentioned we are. So, why beat yourself up? Why judge yourself for judging others? And, in fact, if you could just stop judging your own life, you wouldn't be judging anyone else's.

The problem is not that we make judgments, but that we believe the judgments we make, just as we believe our own stories. But, just like our stories, judgments simply come from the made-up meaning we internally create, and therefore, can't be right or wrong – they are just made up, based on our perceptions and beliefs of the world. Sure, you judge others and even as you spiritually evolve, you will likely continue to judge others, but do you have to believe everything you tell yourself? There is a part of you that can discern, and not believe everything you think. This is the same part of you that can question your stories and the meanings you give to experience.

Spiritual Myth -
You must never judge anyone

What would happen if this wise part of you stopped seeing yourself as someone who is judgmental and started seeing yourself as someone who is able to make assessments, and make conscious and healthy choices, based on those assessments? And, when you found yourself in real judgment of another, you recognized that judgment as being a reflection of your own self-judgment – your own stories.

Once we recognize that our judgment of another is really about judging our self, we have the opportunity to learn - and shift something inside of us. We can look for the beliefs that created the judgment in the first place. And, when

we take responsibility for them and don't take them so serious, we can allow the beliefs to loosen just a little, until eventually they are completely gone. We know when we have moved past self-judgment because one day we realize that we no longer judge others for their once perceived differences or shortcomings. The "work" is not to stop judging others, but to embrace and love our own humanness and divinity, equally and unconditionally.

What three judgments do you often think about others?

What can you learn about yourself from these judgments?

Ego Be Gone!

Once we find the dance between ego and soul, our lives take on a magical rhythm that makes everything possible.

Does it seem impossible to get rid of your ego no matter how hard you try? That's because it *is* impossible. Having an ego and being human go hand-in-hand. We need our egos in order to live, survive, and even thrive on this planet. Our ego is a great gift that we are given from the time we are born until the time we die. The ego gets a lot of bad press spiritually speaking, but it's not only a good thing, it is essential. Trying to get rid of the ego is like trying to stop breathing, it's impossible.

Just how much control your ego has over your life and your choices, is another thing altogether.

Unless we become conscious of the ego's part in our life, and we monitor it's control, it can sooner or later run the show. The ego is a tool, to be used, to navigate through life. Without the ego, we would not survive as humans, and we wouldn't even care if we survived or not.

The problem, with having an ego, is that unless put in its place, it will take charge, and if we deny it, like a small child, it will scream louder until heard.

The question is "does the ego lead or does it follow?" When our egos lead our lives, we usually end up with the need to control everything and experience a lot of fear, worry and anxiety in most aspects of our lives, as well as friction and disconnection in our relationships. Another symptom that our egos are leading our lives is when our self esteem is only based on how much we acquire or accomplish in life.

When we become aware of the ego, and ask it to follow rather than lead, the ego can relax its hold on our lives and not work so hard. When a higher wisdom or consciousness is welcomed into our life, we can begin to hand over our power to what is eternally grand and knowing, and our egos can relax and do the job of tour guide that they were meant to do.

When our soul-self and ego-self are in proper balance, our egos can give us information about our environment, similar to that of a semi-knowledgeable tour guide. Tour guides don't have any power to control us – they simply share information and make suggestions, but at any time we can get off the bus and change the journey.

Managing our ego-guide is the job of our internal gate keeper, who is aware of all parts of us and can soothe the ego, and ask it to step back and take the role of tour guide, rather than dictator. At the same time, our internal gate keeper can direct us towards our intuitive powers, and the wisdom of our inner knowing.

Spiritual Myth -
You must release your ego to grow spiritually

Our inner wisdom, combined with the tour guiding skills of our ego, are an unstoppable duo and can support a path of great understanding and worldly success. Once we find the dance between ego and soul, our lives take on a magical rhythm that makes everything possible.

Describe how your life is ego driven?

If you were to embrace greater faith, in a higher wisdom and trusted your intuitive powers, how much could your ego relinquish control? What would change in your life?

PURPOSE!

Whenever I do workshops, I always ask, "Who here knows their purpose". Often, not a hand goes up. But when I ask, "how many of you believe you have a purpose?' Every single person raises their hand. If we all believe we have a purpose, why is it that so few of us know what it is?

We all have a deep sense of who we really are. It is this intuitive sense which guides us to the knowing that we have a purpose. It is also this intuitive sense that can guide us to knowing what it is, and to experiencing it in our lives. But, a funny thing happens on the way to discovering our purpose; we stop listening. Really, it is that simple. We stop listening to our intuitive senses when it comes to uncovering and living our purpose.

During one of my workshops, a man asked me how to find out what his purpose was. He said he had no idea and could never figure it out for himself. I asked him the simplest of questions, "What would you do if you didn't have to worry about money or anything else?" Without a second's hesitation, his face lit up and he responded "I'd move to the country and start a farm". When I suggested to him that his purpose was speaking to him through this great desire, he suddenly started arguing about all the reasons he couldn't follow his heart. This is exactly what we all do. We have given so much attention to all the reasons why we can't follow our hearts that we don't even hear it calling to us anymore. If we still do hear it, we minimize it, and somehow make it impossible or even wrong to entertain the thought and follow our higher senses.

Our purpose speaks to us through our desires and inspiration. When we have inspiration to do something in our lives, it is our higher wisdom speaking to us. It might not make any sense, and may seem completely impossible - which is even more of a reason to listen to the voices in our hearts, because when it seems unreasonable or impossible to follow our desires, we know that voice didn't come from us. It came from a higher power – the part of us who knows our greatest possible destiny. Virtually everybody knows what they would want to do if it weren't for all the obstacles which seem to prevent them from even dreaming the dream.

No matter what you choose to do with your life – it is perfect. You can keep living a life that focuses around survival and playing it safe, or you can choose to start listening to that voice that calls you. The voice that says, "paint, move to the country, sing, start your own business, or write a book". That voice is present inside you. It might only tell you the very next step, but when you follow that step and the one after that and one after that, you will one day wake up living the life of your dreams – living your purpose.

You are right – you have a purpose. And that purpose is alive and waiting for you to start listening and stop making excuses. I don't care what your excuse is – it is all bogus. When you are given an inspiration and you have the guts to follow it, the universe will conspire to support your dream in ways you could never have imagined - making all your obstacles disappear (or useful in your journey). You are not alone in fulfilling your purpose. The universe supports you in all that you desire, but first you must consciously choose to walk the path of the unknown, and have faith that the messages in your heart are the divine guidance you have been awaiting.

If nothing stopped me and success was guaranteed, I would: (describe the greatest possibility of your life):

GOD PRAYS TO YOU

Have you considered that God prays to you?

Every intuitive thought or feeling you have is a message from God. Every time you have a sense to do something that doesn't make sense or a little feeling that directs you in a way you never would have thought of yourself, it is God speaking to you. The very thing that you want to do with your life is God communicating with you. It's a beautiful cycle; God whispers in your ear "Write a book to help people". You have an overwhelming feeling you want to write a book to help people. But you have fear and reservations so you start praying back to God; "God, help me to write this book." You are actually praying back to God, what God has already prayed to you. God wants for you what you want for yourself. It really is that simple.

What might God be praying to you about?

CLICK: EMOTIONALLY FAST FORWARDING!

If we wait only for the perfect moments to be present, we miss life.

In the movie "Click", the character played by Adam Sandler had the ability to fast forward through any undesirable event in his life just by clicking a remote control. Before he knew it, he had fast forwarded through his whole life – missing all the experiences he didn't want to feel, but also missing all the wonderful experiences, as well. In the end, they became the same. He realized that, not only did he miss all the joy in his life, but also, *he missed life,* and without the whole-of-life (the good and bad), the joy was void.

It takes *the full experience of life* to know joy, peace, love and connection. If we just wait for the perfect moments, when we can experience only what we claim as good, we can't really experience the fullness of any moment or any emotion. Could you know what joy was without first feeling its opposite? What about love, peace or freedom? Without contrast, our experience of life becomes flat and without body. It takes the full experience of life, to know who we are, and to participate in this great adventure called our lives.

If we wait only for the perfect moments to be present, we miss life.

Like Adam Sandler, we unknowingly fast forward through our lives, every time we deny an experience, alter our feelings artificially or repress the totality of our experience. Ironically, we also miss the very thing we are looking for. When we emotionally fast forward through life, it disconnects us from our center and creates a feeling of being lost or alone. It is by being fully present (without a story) in the wholeness of each moment, that we move back into our center and find connection with our god-selves, and as a result, unlimited joy and peace fill us from the inside out – uninfluenced by the human experience we might be having. We experience the knowingness of who we are beyond all human chaos and challenge. It is in these moments that we express our greatest spiritual selves in human

form, and our divinity – like all great spiritual beings – shines through.

In every moment, you have the opportunity to experience and express your greatest spiritual self, just by being present, without a story, in the every-day chaos, challenge and gift of the life you are now living. This is your invitation.....

What life events have you fast forwarded through? What did you honestly miss?

____

____

____

____

____

____

____

What life events are you now fast forwarding through?

How might you become present in all moments of your life?

Enlightenment Is Inevitable...

...but living life to the fullest is optional. We are meant to live, experiencing everything we can and enjoying this amazing gift of life – to the greatest possible extent. We are meant to love and touch and experiment with the great possibilities of who we really are, and what we can create. We are meant to swing from the highest swing, ski down the grandest peak and fly with the birds around the world in fast planes or hot air balloons. We are given great freedom to choose just how much or how little adventure we want to experience. And, if we choose to spend our entire lives in a small town, raising a family and spending long nights in front of a roaring fire, with the people we love, or just reading a book by ourselves, that too is grandly wonderful.

Being spiritual doesn't have a set of rules or guidelines. There is no right or wrong way to be spiritual. It's all good. There is no need to judge any experience in your life – no matter how painful or how much you think you screwed up.

These experiences are part of the journey, and can one day unfold into a purposeful life. Life dances between chaos and creation, and in fact, chaos is a creator. Inner turmoil moves us to find answers, and often those answers lead us to find what we are looking for – be that a happier relationship, a better job, a healthier body, freedom, abundance, or our life's purpose.

Every day of your life, you get a blank canvas to create and re-create your greatest dream, of your grandest life. You are the artist of your life, and you get to choose how that life is lived. No matter how stuck you might feel, at any given moment, you get to choose again, simply by changing the story and dreaming a new dream into creation.

Whether you acknowledge it now or not, you and only you are the master and creator of the life you have lived, and the life that flows in front of you. *In the art of being human, can you discover what it means to be the greatest expression of you?* Can you embrace the gift of yourself and have the courage to explore and express all your gifts, and choose a purpose that sets you free and allows you to discover the potential that lies within, burning with desire to be unlocked. Can you embrace

your humanness, by having the courage to laugh at yourself and the stories you have made up? Can you stop taking yourself so seriously, and just explore the journey of being human, all the while knowing beyond a shadow of a doubt, you are God. And, if you can't yet accept that you are God, accept that God loves you and wants, more than anything, for you to love and accept yourself unconditionally, no matter where you are in the wonderful journey of your life. The only job you have to do is *just be,* and express the gloriousness of who you really are. After that – everything else takes care of itself.

Now, it's time to celebrate – simply for being alive.

Letter From God

You are light. You are love. Of all my children, you are blessed with special and unique gifts. Through all your trials and tribulations, you have done well and learned much. You beam with the knowledge and wisdom of your being.

With dreams in hand, you will go forward and create all you and I have planned and intended for you. Your path in life is to be a source of love and inspiration to all those you touch. You are guided, my child, every step of the way. Do not doubt my love for you. I am within and wherever you might venture. There is no fear so great that cannot be removed with my love. Bring faith unto me (all your troubles and woes) and I will heal you as you go about your daily life and heal others in my light.

You ask what you need to do to fulfill your destiny. All you need to do is remember that you are love, and each small step in the name of love is a step towards your greatest destiny of all. Be patient - all will come. Live each moment fully alive and vibrant, and the rest will come my child - the rest will come.

Love,
God

ABOUT THE AUTHOR

Nanice Ellis grew up in New York but after falling in love with Utah's beautiful mountains and adventurous activities moved to Salt Lake City, Utah in 1997 - where she now lives with her three extraordinary children: Dustin, Travis and Clay and her beautiful daughter-in-law April.

Nanice is an international Life Coach and motivational speaker, who specializes in spirituality and guiding others to discover their intrinsic power and living their dreams.

Nanice is also the author of "The Infinite Power of You", "Is There a White Elephant in Your Way?", and "What If...". Through her coaching, writing and motivational seminars, she lives her greatest purpose, which is helping others find their own purpose.

Nanice loves traveling the world, finding answers and discovering even more questions. During the winter, you will find Nanice skiing the amazing slopes of Utah and in the summer, you'll find her wake boarding on Lake Powell, hiking, mountain biking or exploring some amazing new possibilities.

For more information on Nanice,

please visit www.Nanice.com

Books By Nanice

- The Infinite Power of You!
- Zest Point
- Out of The Jungle
- Even Gandhi Got Hungry and Buddha Got Mad!
- LipPrints
- What *if*...
- The Gratitude Journal
- I Am

Nanice is available for Workshops, Presentations nd Keynotes, as well as Tele-conferencing and)ne-on-One Coaching sessions.

Visit www.Nanice.com for current adio show times, podcasts, insightful rticles, life enhancement quizzes, free ownloads and to order more books!

WWW.NANICE.COM

Nanice@Nanice.com

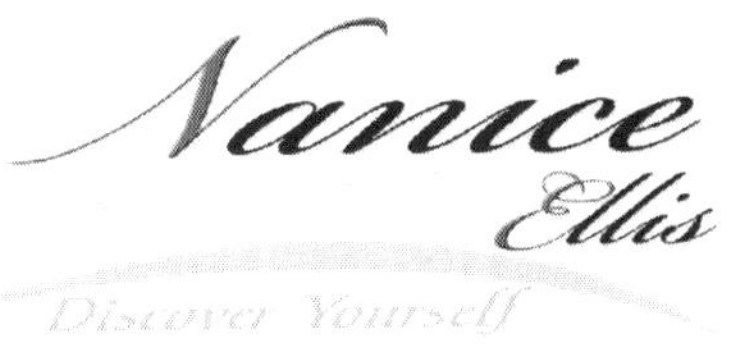

Made in the USA
Middletown, DE
06 October 2015